STOP WORRYING

&

START LIVING

Conquer Negative Thinking, Declutter Your Mind, Relieve Stress & Anxiety, and Lead a Happy and Successful Life

Pollux Andrews

polluxandrews@gmail.com

Other Books by Author

Discipline Yourself: Overcome Self-Sabotaging Behavior, Build Habits and Systems to Boost Willpower, and Thrive Your Way To Success

Table of Contents:

Introduction	*3*
Chapter 1: Why Clutter Your Mind?	*7*
Chapter 2: Stop Worrying	*24*
Chapter 3: Making Negative Thinking An Anathema	*35*
Chapter 4: Relax!	*46*
Chapter 5: Staying Energized At Work And Your Life	*58*
Chapter 6: Stress And Success	*68*
Chapter 7: Leveraging Stress For A Happier Life	*80*
Conclusion	*94*

Introduction

"There's more to life than increasing its speed." - Mahatma Gandhi

Man is the architect of his thoughts. Have you noticed that when you surround yourself with an atmosphere of negative cosmic energy that things seem to happen just as you thought they would pan out?

Stress in itself does not have enough fingers to grab us without our consent; one way or the other, we give it air to breathe into our lives and make a nest for it. You may have to fight wars of pressure both on personal fronts and professional fronts, having to cope with managerial and leadership duties, family responsibilities, and so on. They all have the potentials of causing stress.

But do you really need to feel stressed?

Having a stressful outlook is not economical to your body psyche.
When you are stressed, the propensity to smile is reduced and frowning or a moody face becomes the reoccurring decimal. The next time you feel stressed, smile and remember

that it is <u>much easier to smile</u> than to frown which is caused by stress. Smiling is much more economical for you.

We may visualize stress as the heat that emanates from a running machine, and in that light, we can easily associate it with almost everybody. Yes, it is something everyone has got to deal with. However, although stress might be a general experience many people have in the course of running their daily lives, what's not general are the actions individuals take to mitigate the tendency for stress to take any significant toll on them.

Stress can truly act as barriers to the efficient discharge of our daily duties, both personally and in our corporate spheres. When we are stressed, we often feel that congestion of mind, which leads to poor thought patterns, and even sharply reduced productivity.

Mahatma Gandhi came to a profound realization that the true and noble codes of life can afford you living without stressors poking you around, yet, guarantees you success at the tunnel's end. However, it is important to emphasize that this does not happen by speeding up your life unnecessarily. There is the need for an individual to think coherently and in clarity, make reasonable conclusions as to what directions to take and take the required steps. By rushing everything, you have a higher tendency of running into the welcoming arms of stressors than into success.

So the very underlining point is the need for equilibrium, understanding the art of striking balances. The absence of stress management skills has the consequence of exposing yourself to physical and psychological attacks from stress. And what follows naturally after that is a downward-leaning life that does not promise a lot of results in every aspect; depression and other effects that constitute friction to efficient living sets in.

As soon as you figure out you are under stress, the most recommended way out is adopting stress management strategies. One thing is that if stress dominates you for too long, the effects are worse than diseases; it can eat up both your physical body and your zest towards productivity and success altogether. Now, that is dangerous, especially for millennials and youths.

It is <u>a fact</u> that individuals under stress face challenges managing their environment efficiently as well as themselves and almost everything they do. So if you think of it, what is the essence of living at all if one cannot do anything with excellence?

It turns out that stressors make an army that would fight us at every opportunity they have to do so.

In this book, you will find those subtle tips that you need to win the war against stress, decongest your mind, and leverage on that to mitigate negative thought behaviors, worries, undue anxieties, and very importantly, RELAX. We will critically x-ray all the viable means that will keep us ever-smiling and live a successful life.

At the end of it all, productivity and efficiency are the goals we hope to score.

Chapter 1: Why Clutter Your Mind?

Clutter is the physical manifestation of unmade decisions fueled by procrastination. Christina Scalise

Well, it is only natural that we don't leave all the documents, coffee cups, and stationery all jam-packed on our office tables; we sort them out and organize them. Similarly, we declutter our homes to retain a structure that reflects organization and elegance; these are the qualities we also radiate from our minds when we do not clutter.

The questions you must answer for yourself are: Why do I clutter my mind? Why do I procrastinate in making decisions about my life?

You often want to keep your to-do list, important dates, and procedures for carrying out several processes in your mind and when you miss any of them, you feel like the world has spun you into a hole of nothingness. **Read this** - you are not the only one going through this and instead of mourning the fact that you cluttered your mind with one thing or the other which led to forgetfulness, the best thing is to read on and apply the great things you will learn herein.

It requires some good level of dedication to declutter your mind and it pays off in the long run. You get more strongly connected to your environment and increase your chances of getting a perfect shot at a successful life.

In conducting your daily life, you need a balance, and this balance emanates from your central seat of being—the mind. Whirling around in your mind causes instabilities that you are likely not ready to manage, and consequently, you expose yourself to the mercies of forces that may cause you harm.

Now, in a more scientific perspective, the brain is where the thought processes and mental activities take place. Neurons fire electrical impulses here and there when we think, commit things to memory, or overload ourselves with information. The pieces of the brain that coordinates trauma, depression, bad memories and so on are still under the study of science and so, we should not expect a miracle decluttering our minds overnight based on science. But we have a role to play;

to apply the basic pieces of stuff that we are aware are before us.

Decluttering your mind is not rocket science, however, it is not trivial. Just give it a little commitment and that is all that it would need.

There are three courses of action that would be recommended for relieving your mind of worries. They turn out to be things people do unconsciously and independently in their daily lives. We will look into them after we briefly consider some factors that can cause the mind to get cluttered up.

FACTORS THAT CAN LEAD TO A CLUTTERED MIND

- Routine Stress

There are stressors that seem to be integrated into the way we run our day-to-day lives. In this century, there is a heavy mass of information flowing around and that can become overwhelming for some of us. You get to see saddening headlines making the front page, hear about the low employment rate, global warming, terrorism, and viral ailments, and much more. These can become daunting especially when one is in the middle of these issues and in the long run, can cause health issues, insomnia, panics, worries, and depression. With all these matters constantly clogging the human mind, it starts rusting off and causing problems.

- Multiple Options

They say beggars have no choice; however, an extremely wide array of options and choices can cause one to have the stint of dizziness. In today's world, we now have very large shops and this can make it difficult to actually make specific choices. It has a way of psychologically influencing our lives by causing undue anxieties and indecisions. So many alternatives don't necessarily translate into a life of success, rather, it could plague our thinking and strain our decision-making muscles.

- So many activities and things

Chances are that you always have to answer the messages left you on your social media handles, take calls, check out your wardrobe as to what clothes to put on, look out for toys for the kids, shop for your needs, go to work, attend some social functions, and these can pile up and constitute a yoke that causes stress and anxiety. You want to meet with all these demands the best way possible. The consequence of this is that you have to work your ass off and keep your mind constantly ruminating one action after the other.

TIPS FOR DECLUTTERING THE MIND

It is true that the tips here might seem trivial and easy to come by, however, an application of the instructions would convince you of their potency.

- Take a few deep Breaths

This is quite a simple exercise to do, but it is also as effective as it is simple. Just take a couple of deep breaths, count and focus on them for some minutes. Pay keen attention to your breathing rhythm and monitor your inhales and exhales. This exercise has a therapeutic effect on the mind and helps it stay put on a thought without swaying about. The focus on the rhythm carves a flow of thought that keeps the mind away from all forms of distraction.

- Learn the art of Writing

Let the paper hold all the information that seems to mess up your mind. By writing down the things on your mind on paper, you relieve your mind of the load of carrying too much information. You also get a clearer picture of your thoughts and can easily articulate your ideas. Putting down your thoughts also makes it easier for you to recall what you thought about.

- Itemise the relevant things you have thought of

A good step towards decluttering your mind is making a specific note of those things you think of that are of the most importance to you. Sift through all the things you have littering your mind and make a sort of scale for them categorizing them in order of relevance.

- Remove

The fictional character Sherlock Holmes once said, *"Once you eliminate every impossibility, whatever remains, no matter how improbable, must be the truth."* In the same light, you can strike some things off your list until you have a list that contains all the important things in your mind. It will help you rid your mind of unnecessary thoughts.

You could even have a long list up in your head that you didn't write down. How do you remove this from your subconscious and get on with your life? You can do this by knowing that whatever you believe is what you will always get. Just believe the thought is not there and that worry will naturally be removed. The act of belief doesn't require spatial science to execute it.

- Sleep Well

Your sleeping pattern could also be a huge contributor to the cluttering of your mind. The fatigue that comes with irregular and unhealthy sleeping behaviors does little to help our mind articulate thoughts. Lack of sleep, like malnutrition, affects your mind and overall body health. It is a good idea to take interest in developing a good sleep pattern. According to Natural Patterns of Sleep, our bodies require sleep in order to maintain proper function and health.

- Do some minor Physical Exercises

Try jogging in the morning, take a long walk, or engage in some other light exercises. They are highly effective in refreshing the mind and decongesting it of numerous thoughts or in some cases, they pattern the thoughts for you. It has an effect that sort of relieves the mind's muscles.

- Do not watch too much Television

Yea! Some persons might be wondering what the heck it is that TV has to do with an overloaded mind, but it does. The noise, unnecessary information, and so on does not help to stabilize the mind. Consider relaxing with music instead or do some light reading; they would instill some quiet into the mind that you would be ever grateful for.

Do you know about the recommendations of <u>The American Academy of Pediatrics</u>?

Do not feel bamboozled by what you read next on their recommendations. Many of us are guilty but we could learn and make corrections.

Among their recommendations are:

1. Children younger than 18 months should avoid the use of screen media other than video-chatting. Parents who have kids from 18 to 24 months of age who want to introduce digital media should choose high-quality programming, and watch it with their children to help them understand what they're seeing.
2. For children aged 2 to 5 years, the use of the screen must be limited to 1 hour per day of high-quality programs. Parents should co-view media with children to help them understand what they are seeing and apply it to the world around them.
3. For children aged 6 and **older**, there should be consistent limits on the time spent using media and the types of media, and make sure media does not take the place of **adequate sleep, physical activity and other behaviors essential to health.**
4. Designate media-free times together, such as dinner or driving, as well as media-free locations at home, such as bedrooms.
- Appreciate the freshness of Nature

Go to the fountains, climb some mountains, just do something that would provoke an admiration of nature in you. It helps you take your mind off multiple thoughts and calmly guides your thinking pattern.

Always try to go out on weekends to wonderful places with a friend, your family or even solo by yourself.

- Cheer up as often as you can

Laugh and do not be weighed down. There can hardly be a better medicine than that. It refreshes your emotions and mind and brings out the optimal performance you have got. Laughing helps you calm the storms of thoughts raging in your mind.

Life is short to be *too serious* after all, so why not cheer up; they say no matter how serious you take life, you will never make it out alive. So, laugh at some jokes, feel the warmth of fine comedy, go on outings with friends and catch some high-flying fun, consider going to the movies. No matter how deep the root of the stress is, it would be uprooted.

- Cut down your To-Do List

The magicians often say "the more you look, the less you see." The same magic also applies to life and activities as well. The less you have on your list of To-Dos, the more focused you tend to be and the more effective you become at achieving them. So, it is good practice to make a To-Do List with less content and then focus on achieving the items on the list. It would help to keep your thinking in perspective.

- Workout

Go to the gym, run, and do some exercise. Aside from the fact that you will get your body in great shape, you sweat and your body undergoes metabolisms that enhances its overall performance—from the rhythm of your heart to the swinging of your moods, and the robust effect of energy utilization within it.

The more bodily activity you engage in, the better for you. It would sharpen the mental capacity as much as it would elevate your health balance.

- Take things at your pace, No Hurrying

There is something about taking things step-by-step. Walking, speaking, and going about life at a slow pace can change the entire configuration of the mind. It sends the signal that you do not wish to live your life by the timeframes set up by other people, you want to take control of your life and live it exactly the way you want to. Consequently, your mind becomes less disorderly.

- Relieve the mind of Grudges

Worry never solves the problem, it actually delays the solution. When you keep bad memories in your mind, when you are frustrated, you tend to burden your mind with so many unnecessary weights. Yes, it might be difficult to control, yes, it might be emotional and natural, however, it is not out of control. Get rid of the grudges that are harbored within you. Learn to "let it go."

- Decongest Your Environment

You might not know this, but analytical minds constantly work to ensure that they keep a record of what and where things are. So, in a highly cluttered environment, there is the pressure on the mind to keep track of the position of things and that does little to help the mind retain its organization.

- Avoid Multitasking

While multitasking can be a desirable quality, don't forget the maxim "jack of all trades, master of none." It is a common problem with multi-taskers that they fail to attain maximum result because they distribute their mind across too wide a number of matters. So, try focusing and elevating your productivity one task at a time. After one task, then you go on to the other, and so on, until you reach your goals for every task you have in mind.

- Let others in on Your Thoughts

They say a problem shared is half solved. This is no truer anywhere than when you are in the game of decluttering your mind. You can share your thoughts with others; it can help you in reaching conclusions on certain issues faster and more efficiently. You might have that person who makes your day, that you feel comfortable with, that you can share your troubles with. Please do so and bring relief to your mind.

- Use a Journal

There is no better friend for your mind than your notepad. Using a journal helps you record and analyze your thoughts. This activity helps shape your style of thinking as well as trims out negative thinking. Studies are indicating that this exercise frees up mental space and creates room in your mind for more information to come in and be processed. Getting a bit technical, journalizing improves the processing capacity of your mind and sends stress packing. You can also release the gases of depression from your mind by putting things down in a journal, and it is also easy to do. You don't have to be a Nobel Laureate to write in your journal; it's not rocket science, so get writing and improve the environment of your mind

- Cultivate the ability to let things go

You can reduce the effects of stress on you by moving on and accepting yourself for who you are. They say people fall a thousand times, but great people rise up a thousand and one times. Be courageous and face life without ruining your temperament and mental acuity. Censor your mind to repel the negative and attract the positive. Learn to love yourself and feed your esteem and self-worth.

- Reduce the Volume of time you Spend on the Media

Spending too much time on the internet and media can be daunting and can have an effect on the ecosystem of your mind. Spending so much time online, on social media or even watching viral videos on YouTube can cause your brain to possess an information overload which consequently leads to stress and anxiety. Consciously cut down on your intake of media information, or more so, select and carefully choose what you wish to learn from the internet each day. Stay away from contents that have a negative impact on your overall mental health. How do you sieve the information you should welcome? If it does not make you relieved and organized mentally, if it does not help you accomplish the goals you have prioritized in your mind, it is not worth the time.

- Shut down for a Moment

Fold up your laptop—it's an enemy, switch off your mobile phones, take a deep sleep, take a stroll in the ambiance of fresh air and flowing winds that massage your body, keep your mind in a passive mode for a moment.

There is always a time for auditing in every organization; run through your mind and identify the needed and the unnecessary, eliminate the thoughts you do not need. Give yourself that big break you deserve. If your mind had mouths, it would say a million "thank yous" to you for it.

WHAT YOU GAIN BY DECLUTTERING YOUR MIND

Decluttering your mind comes with a number of good packages as well. Some of them include:

- You start to develop concentration skills
- You start developing creativity
- Your sleeping pattern begins to improve
- You start to experience better moods
- You soon realize that you are not so attached to the past

- You begin to understand the essence of timing and the need to avoid procrastination

Chapter 2: Stop Worrying

"Worry is the interest paid on trouble before it is due" – William R. Inge

Worry is the feeling we have when we are anxious about a problem we are not in control of. It is said that you should do your best and leave the rest, but the human mind will always worry about what is next, that's why we are always afraid to start something. It is not because we don't have ideas, but the fear of failure, the fear of what people will think of us. The human mind can be pessimistic as much as we want to be optimistic, we fear for what will happen next. We put ourself in a box and that is why we worry.

According to the Bureau of Standards, "A dense fog covering seven city blocks, to a depth of 100 feet, is composed of something less than one glass of water." So, if all the fog covering seven city blocks, 100 feet deep, were collected and held in a single drinking glass, it would not even fill it. Now, this could be compared to our worries. If we can see into the future and if we could see our problems in their true light, they wouldn't tend to blind us to the world, to living itself, but instead, could be relegated to their true size and place. And if all the things most people worry about were reduced to their true size, you could probably put them all into a drinking glass, too.

Opinions aren't facts, stop worrying about what people think of you because, they are not your reality.

100% fact about worry (The worry chart) is that 40% never happens, 30% concerns the past, 12% are needless health concerns, 10% are insignificant and petty issues, and 8% are the actual legitimate concerns. According to this fact, we worry mainly about situations that are not visible, current and are irrelevant.

Summary: It's easy to see that worry and anxiety, for the most part, are a <u>waste of our time</u> and have a very negative effect on our life and the life of those to whom we might bring an aptly spoken word of counsel.

Factors That Can Lead to Worry

- Overthinking

Overthinking is an act of creating problems that are not there. It is replaying the negative roles and making them affect the present and future possibilities without you even trying to get the best out of it.

Overthinking is the biggest cause of unhappiness. Keep yourself occupied.

Be aware of your thought process and consciously try to think of positive outcomes instead of negative ones and this can reduce your worries.

- Insecurity

Don't let the fear of insecurity stop you from trying new things.

Uncertainty can lead to insecurity which can lead to vulnerability and low self-esteem.

Oftentimes, insecurity comes from past traumas, recent experiences of rejection and failure. When you doubt yourself, you become less confident in yourself and become insecure.

It is okay to be insecure at some point because we are humans and flawed. However, when you stay doubting yourself it is bad. Love yourself and good things will come your way.

- Stress

Anxiety is a reaction to stress and stress can lead to health problems such as depression, insomnia, sickness etc. When the body is stressed, it generates hormones such as cortisol which helps to deal with stressful situations.

Stress occurs when you have too much going on for you or you simply cohabit with the fear of the unknown. You need to relax, exercise the bod, and mind to get over stress.

As at 2017, an estimated <u>85% of millennial's</u> report being stressed due to financial and job-related concerns. 75% of Gen X'ers and Boomers are more likely to report being stressful than just the 62% matures.

The top 7 causes of stress in America include Job Pressure, Money, Health, Relationships, Poor Nutrition, Media overload and Sleep Deprivation.

- Too much responsibility

The greatest weapon against stress is the ability to choose one thought over the other.

Trying to be a perfectionist brings increased stress. There is just so much you can handle and if you go past that, you tend to injure yourself, be it physically or mentally. Learn to make your priorities right to avoid being stressed. The important principle/ Eisenhower's urgent time management principle is one to look at.

- Past events

Past events are the key source of stress in a person. Past traumas will forever be there no matter how hard we try to push them aside from our thought and this simply brings one to being stressed.

Health Consequences of Worry

- Depression

Depression is the loss of interest in activities. When you worry too much, you tend to become absent-minded to the things that matter at some point. Depression is a mental health disorder with symptoms ranging from loss of appetite to weight loss and can be treated through psychotherapy or drug treatment.

Depression symptoms should be taken seriously as it can lead to death if neglected.

- Insomnia

Insomnia is a sleep disorder characterized by lack of sleep even when you want to and can lead to a migraine and nausea. Some of the symptoms of insomnia include discomfort and stress and can be treated by practicing a good sleeping pattern or consultation with your doctor for the use of a sleeping pill or other prescriptions.

- Irritability

This is the change of the state of a person, from being alright to being easily upset at little things, especially in a stressful situation. People often call it mood swing, which occurs mostly when a girl is ovulating some days before her period starts or bipolar disorder which is when a person drastically changes his/her attitude towards something.

This can affect people around you and thus it's toxic, however, it can be treated by meditating.

- Nausea

Nausea is the uneasiness a person feels in the stomach. It is quite discomforting and can be treated by simply seeing a doctor for advice and getting prescriptions or by trying to rest when stressed.

- Muscle Tension

Muscle tension occurs when the body is tensed up due to an excessive strain in posture. This is another very familiar symptom of stress and can be relieved by resting well, exercising, massage or medical intervention.

Other symptoms that can affect you when you stress yourself and engage in worry include:

- Obesity

Obesity is a disorder where a person has accumulated so much fat that it becomes a major health problem. Obesity is caused when you eat too much and this can be as a result of being idle or overthinking.

- Heart disease

This is a term that is generally used to classify all diseases that affect the heart. Quitting smoking and exercising regularly can help prevent heart disease. There are various types of heart disease and their symptoms range from profuse sweating, and nausea to body pain.

- Weight loss

Weight loss is the reduction in body mass of a person. It could be healthy and unhealthy depending on the main purpose, negative thinking stresses the body to an extent that we see these symptoms and it may not be healthy because we lose fluids that are supposed to help revive the body and if not given attention, can lead to illness.

- High blood pressure

This is a condition in which the force of the blood against the artery walls is too high and the acute source of high blood pressure is stress. It can also happen on its own and if not taken care of immediately, it can lead to heart attack, stroke, kidney disease, etc.

How to control or limit your worry

- Engage in Positive Thinking

Your positive action combined with your positive thinking results in success. - **Shiv Khera**

Have a positive mentality by making the energy around you positive. A happy mind is a healthy mind. Do away with negative energy that will make you see the worse in every situation and focus on the present. Turn failure into lessons. You can't know all and when you fail, you rise up and try again and learn from it. It can be discomforting but it is worth every penny.

- Appreciating yourself

Appreciate yourself always. The first step to forgiving others and letting go of situations and circumstances is by loving yourself. It wouldn't hurt if you take yourself out on a treat and be grateful for the gift of life, it could be way worse but if it isn't, learn to make lemonade when life gives you a lemon and learn to be kind to yourself.

- Embrace uncertainty

You have to accept and come to terms with the fact that there is an inherent degree of uncertainty in humans. Although theorists have been making efforts to understand the tricks and randomness and chaos, it still remains an unmoved fact that there are uncertainties in the formulation of many things we would experience in the course of our lives.

- Face your fear

We worry because we are scared of what the future holds and we find new ways in our head to avoid the situation. You cannot be successful in every situation if you don't pass through it to learn to face your fears. There can only be two possible outcomes when you pass through situations, it could be either a success story or failure.

Worrying cannot be completely eliminated but we can learn to control our emotions and thoughts. See the good in everything and if it does not turn out in your favor, try again.

- Take care of your body

A healthy body is a healthy mind so take care of your body. Exercise daily and eat good food. Eating good improves your overall health and also feeds your body with the nutrients it needs while exercise enhances your physical fitness and also helps to avoid health issues. Exercise 3-5 times a week to feel the effect on your body.

As a remark, it is okay to worry; in fact, it is part of the human mind to be overprotective and sense danger even before it is there. When you understand this, you will be able to take the step of identifying what to control and influence. You can't always control your emotions but you can prevent the outburst by focusing on what you can control, which is your attitude and the way you respond to the situation.

Stop worrying about all that could occur tomorrow. You are getting agitated about things that haven't happened yet and may never happen. Stay here, right here, in this moment. What is going on right now, what is occurring right here, that is all that matters, that is where your life is being lived. - **Neale Donald Walsch**

Chapter 3: Making Negative Thinking An Anathema

"Don't feed your mind with negative thoughts. If you do, you will come to believe them". - Catherine Pulsifer

Negative thinking is the process where you find yourself assuming the worse in a situation and getting worked up about it. It is necessary to have these feelings as we are humans and we have the urge to protect ourselves against the unknown but the ability to control our thought is what makes us strong and emotionally intelligent.

> *If we understand the power of our thoughts, we would guard them more closely. If we understand the power of our words, we will create our own weaknesses and strengths.* ***Betty Eadie***

Our words are very powerful and they can either break you or make you. More often than not, the words that come out from our mouth are from what we think and this can affect a person either positively or negatively.

Thinking can either be positive or negative and according to Robert Schwarz and Gregory Garamoni in their *States of Mind* Model, it proposed a positive-negative mix in thought and for normal people, it was in the ratio of the golden section. That is, 2/3 positive and 1/3 negative. The dose of caution acts as a remedy to overconfidence. This idea has, as we have seen, been shown to be supported by the work of Gabriele Oettingen.

While rational and realistic thinking is supported by a mix of positive and negative thinking, it seems that there are positive benefits of negative thinking and even negative moods.

With the above fact, we can see that not all thoughts are bad but how we control them is what matters. The body will always come up with various bad scenarios that can occur in a situation to make the body prepare for the worse outcomes.

Another fact is that your mood is affected by 90% of what you think. One negative thought can ruin a good mood.

You need to make negative thinking your anathema, which is something you dislike or want to do away with in order to grow and live an almost stress-free life.

Factors That Lead to Negative Thinking

- Self- judgment

Self- judgment is the process of forming an opinion of you. That is evaluating you from an evidence or situation you see. We need to judge our self sometimes to know our worth and how far we have come and and are willing to go. However, you need to let go of negative judgment and wrong evaluation of yourself. It can hinder you from growing to be the best version of yourself and will add to your stress level which will lead you to worry.

We can look at the self-judgment theory to better understand human judgment and how it perceives situations.

Social judgment theory (SJT) is a self-persuasion theory proposed by Carolyn Sherif, Muzafer Sherif, and Carl Hovland and defined by both Sherifs as the perception and evaluation of an idea by comparing it with

Thinking can either be positive or negative and according to Robert Schwarz and Gregory Garamoni in their *States of Mind* Model, it proposed a positive-negative mix in thought and for normal people, it was in the ratio of the golden section. That is, 2/3 positive and 1/3 negative. The dose of caution acts as a remedy to overconfidence. This idea has, as we have seen, been shown to be supported by the work of Gabriele Oettingen.

While rational and realistic thinking is supported by a mix of positive and negative thinking, it seems that there are positive benefits of negative thinking and even negative moods.

With the above fact, we can see that not all thoughts are bad but how we control them is what matters. The body will always come up with various bad scenarios that can occur in a situation to make the body prepare for the worse outcomes.

Another fact is that your mood is affected by 90% of what you think. One negative thought can ruin a good mood.

You need to make negative thinking your anathema, which is something you dislike or want to do away with in order to grow and live an almost stress-free life.

Factors That Lead to Negative Thinking

- Self- judgment

Self- judgment is the process of forming an opinion of you. That is evaluating you from an evidence or situation you see. We need to judge our self sometimes to know our worth and how far we have come and and are willing to go. However, you need to let go of negative judgment and wrong evaluation of yourself. It can hinder you from growing to be the best version of yourself and will add to your stress level which will lead you to worry.

We can look at the self-judgment theory to better understand human judgment and how it perceives situations.

Social judgment theory (SJT) is a self-persuasion theory proposed by Carolyn Sherif, Muzafer Sherif, and Carl Hovland and defined by both Sherifs as the perception and evaluation of an idea by comparing it with current attitudes. <u>According to this theory</u>, an individual weighs every new idea, comparing it with the individual's present point of view to determine where it should be placed on the attitude scale in an individual's mind. SJT is the subconscious sorting out of ideas that occurs at the instant of perception.

- Self- doubt

Self-doubt is the lack of belief in yourself or your capabilities. It is mandatory you fight self- doubt as it can break you and make you have low self-esteem. Believe in yourself and you will see the good that will come out of it.

Doubt kills more dreams than failure will, so, rise up and do away with negative thinking. Understand that not everyone can like you and not every situation will go the way you want it to, but you also need to know that you can go through every circumstance and come out better.

- Habit

Habit is a behavior you adopt too subconsciously and it occurs so regularly that it becomes a routine. Studies have shown that people will perform automated behaviors like pulling out of a driveway or brushing their teeth the same way every single time if they're in the same environment. But if they take a vacation, it's likely that the behavior will change.

Neuroscientists have traced our habit-making behaviors to a part of the brain called the basal ganglia, which also plays a key role in the development of emotions, memories and pattern recognition. <u>Decisions, meanwhile, are made in a different part of the brain called the prefrontal cortex</u>.

- Fear of the unknown

"The oldest and strongest emotion of mankind is fear, and the oldest and strongest kind of fear is fear of the unknown" - ***H.P. Lovecraft, Supernatural_Horror_in Literature***

The fear of the unknown is the greatest fear of all and it can also be known as Xenophobia. It is very difficult to pass through this obstacle because you are always afraid of situations that you have not come across before.

Although very difficult, this obstacle can be passed by first understanding the fear and then learning about it.

- Past Traumas

Trauma can lead to upsetting emotions or memories that won't fade away. These events can leave a person emotionally damaged and somewhat insecure, leading you to have negative thoughts. These emotions cannot be totally ignored but we have to look at the big picture with positivity.

How to Control and Limit Negative Thinking

- Expand your awareness

Fear is what prevents you from expanding your focus. Strengthen your connection to other sectors of your awareness and reduce distraction. This will prevent you from feeding yourself with idle talk or negative feeling. Open your mind and increase your energy frequency by meditating and self-empowerment.

- Observation

"We act how we think and feel. When we remove the negative thought, with it goes the drama and pain." – **Anon.**

Take a seat at the back of your mind and observe your thoughts, identify, acknowledge and filter the negative thoughts that are not necessary and work on the relevant ones.

- Accept your limitations

You need to accept that you are not perfect and cannot be good at everything. We all have strengths and weaknesses and the side you tend to look at will determine where you want to be. You may be athletic and not be book smart, or book smart and not athletic. The rule is this: if you decide to look at your weaknesses all the time, you will break and it will be very difficult to rise up, but if you decide to look at your strengths, you will know that you are better and positive.

- Learn to tame your negative thoughts

Learn to tame your negative thoughts by learning to identify them and by controlling the emotions. Negative thinking is in our head and we are wired to always have that mentality of winning, hence, if things go wrong, we tend to beat ourselves up and it becomes hard to stay positive in that direction which can lead to low self-confidence.

However, we need to control our emotions by self-talking to ourselves which is speaking positively to yourself daily, rethinking your thoughts and snapping back into reality.

- Set realistic expectations

Set expectations that are realistic that you can control. Look at what you have done in the past and then set a goal for the future. In this way, you won't be so hard on yourself because let's face it; when situations don't go your way, you get disappointed but when you know you can do better it reduces the fear.

Stop Thinking Too Much

Overthinking is dwelling on the past events and worrying about what the future holds. Overthinking is the cause of unhappiness and it can ruin you. Often times, a large percentage of our problems would be solved if we stop overthinking things and calm down.

We can control the mind from negative thinking by:

- Looking at a wider perspective

A lot of times, we get caught up with the various situations and circumstances that will cloud our mind and shift our focus from the big picture, but we need to look at things from a wider perspective to be able to grab the root and focus on the issue at hand. The more we look at issues from another angle or outside the box, the more truth we bring into our lives and reduce ignorance.

- Meditation

There is nothing more convenient and comfortable than having inner peace. Focus your mind on a particular object or situation that has brought you peace and success to achieve a mentally clear state. You don't need to go for retreats to clear your mind, you can just focus on the things and people that mean the most to you and watch yourself be a better person.

- Be creative

Be creative; turn your imagination into reality. This is the right time to put those feelings to something that will yield results. An example will be putting those thoughts into words for a person who likes writing, and your expression and story might be what readers need to know and this can be a release for you, too. We've mentioned before that a problem shared is a problem half solved. When you put your emotions and problems into the art of writing, you get them out of your system and better the life of whoever reads your book, as you will be a solution creator.

- Exercise the body

Keep the soul, body and mind healthy by exercising daily to ease stress and reduce fatigue. Exercise enhances and maintains the body's physical fitness and it is performed to help build the body. Also, eat well to prevent health issues and feed the body with nutrients or it will not be able to function properly.

- Talk it out

One of the major problems that causes negative thinking is when you have a lot in your head but you cannot spill it because of what people might think. Declutter your mind, talk to someone or rather, express yourself in words. These mediums can help you tackle the problems and let you find out the root of the problem or situation you have issues with.

In conclusion, we must keep in mind the words of Morihei Ueshiba:

Always keep your mind as bright and clear as the vast sky, the great ocean, and the highest peak, empty of all thoughts. Always keep your body filled with light and heat. Fill yourself with the power of wisdom and enlightenment.

A cluttered mind is too full to receive anything so it keeps pondering on the energy it has and receives. To remove the clutter, we need to connect with our creative mind which can distract us from overthinking.

By making negative thinking your anathema, you have decided to control your situation and do away with bad energy that will influence your life.

Chapter 4: Relax!

"Your mind will answer most questions if you learn to relax and wait for the answer." Williams S. Burroughs

Your mind works tirelessly trying to process information that is relevant and those that are not. Therefore, it is important to relax to help calm the mind and avoid health issues.

According to an <u>October 2007 research by The Mayo Clinic</u>, relaxation must be on the top of everyone's list of priorities. This is true not only for all of you who are workaholics but for stay-at-home moms and everyone who wants to remain in good health. According to the report, relaxation reduces wear and tear on the mind and the body. For example, they state that relaxation reduces blood pressure and heart rate while increasing blood flow to the major muscle. It also reduces back pain, headache and muscle tension while improving concentration. The likelihood of emotional responses such as anger and frustration, which are damaging to the body, are also reduced.

Breathe in, calm your body. Breathe out, smile and relax. Avoid stressing yourself and prevent health issues by refocusing your mind on good things that can help calm the mind and avoid worrying or negative thinking.

A major fact about relaxation is that when you are relaxed, your heart rate is slowed to a slow, resting rate. This gives your heart a chance to rest and gives your body a chance to refresh itself from the stress that it usually carries and also, those who take time to regularly relax, report fewer headaches and pain than those who don't make time to relax.

Relaxation is important and it is a good pain reliever!

How Do You Relax

Relieve the stress on your body and mind by:

- Meditation

Focus your attention on positive thoughts and declutter your mind of the negative energy. This will achieve a mentally clear and calm state making you in control of your emotions. Meditation can help increase productivity because when you are free and have no worries, you tend to execute your daily projects accurately.

- Progressive muscle relaxation

Jacobson's relaxation technique is a type of therapy that focuses on tightening and relaxing specific muscle groups in sequence. It's also known as progressive relaxation therapy. By concentrating on specific areas and tensing and then relaxing them, you can become more aware of your body and physical sensations.

Jacobson's relaxation technique is commonly used to help people with insomnia and people with epilepsy.

- Do something you enjoy

Nothing is too big or small to be done to help you relax. It could be a walk in the park or a stroll in the mall or volunteering or even writing, as it is a form of expression. Letting it all out helps you relax and keeps you refreshed. Doing something you like that can keep you out of work or having you to do serious thinking is what can help you to stay calm.

- Time management

Most of the time, we worry a lot because we don't plan our time well and this is a major way to control the activities around you. Utilize your time well and you get to increase your productivity and to relax to calm your mind and nerves.

> *Until we can manage time, we can manage nothing else.* - **Peter F. Druker**

- Avoid fatigue

We overwork ourselves a lot that we get exhausted and lose focus. It does not always have to be work. Even the traffic within your city is another example of a way we get exhausted and this can lead to health issues like anemia. You can try to avoid fatigue and lift your energy level by:

1. Drinking a lot of water to remain hydrated. Aim to drink eight-ounce glasses of water per day.

2. Eating breakfast. Breakfast is the most important meal of the day as the meal you start your day with can form your day for you and ignoring it can have a side effect in the long run.
3. Take a nap. Do not underrate the power of taking a nap. A 1-2 hours nap can go a very long way to give you a productive day. It also clears your mind and increases your energy level. There are some organizations that allow their staffs to take a short break to nap because they understand the power of taking a nap and what it does to enhance productivity.
4. Take a walk. Exercise is very vital in handling/controlling stress and that is why we have short breaks in school and at work to help us improve our health, productivity, and mood and above all, to keep our focus in check. They say it is better to take the stairs instead of the elevator to enable you to keep moving instead of being in one place. This avenue will also help you clear your mind aside from the fact that it is healthy.
5. Eat food containing iron.Eating a well-balanced meal is important for growth

and also for your health but for now, let's look at the smallest of them all which happens to be very important, iron. Iron carries oxygen to all part of the body and lack of it makes a person weak. Iron is absorbed by the body and releases energy the body needs to be strong and that is why we always have to put salt in our meal, aside from taste it does a lot. Some food rich in iron includes liver, red meat, beans, whole grains, fish, and eggs.

- Listening to good music

Music is therapeutic, a stress reliever, and can put you in a good mood which can help calm you down and also relax. It can also help you to boost your physical health in surprising and astonishing ways. If you take a music lesson or two, that musical lesson can help raise your IQ and even keep you sharp.

Rejuvenate Yourself

Make yourself comfortable and open to new activities. Sometimes, you need to recharge your batteries and go out of your comfort zone, this can be done by:

- Taking a break

"Almost everything will work again if you unplug it for a few minutes...Including you"~ Anne Lamott

Take a break from school, from work to clear your mind- go out to relax, have fun, and experience new things and most of all, make memories. That is why we are given leave and holidays to be able to do these things.

- Go out

Go out, see the world and see the beauty that is in it. Aside from relaxing, it gives you something to think about and do that will be beneficial for your productivity.

- Pamper yourself

Visit a masseuse, go to the mall, buy things for yourself, you deserve some accolade and besides you will have happy memories and lastly relax while at it.

- Get enough sleep

The average sleeping hours for adults range from 5-7 hours and this is because sleep is very vital for our body to get refreshed and also for sanity. Lack of sleep can cause health issues like a headache, high blood pressure, diabetes and so on.

According to a 2010 research paper by UCSD, it is suggested that the secret to a long life lies in getting just enough sleep, which ends up being about 6.5 hours per night. The study looked at the sleeping patterns of 1.1 million persons over the course of 6 years, tracking the amount of sleep each subject averaged alongside their longevity.

Importance of relaxation

It is important to relax because it lowers blood pressure, controls breathing and effectively manages stress.

It is important to relax and improve your health and so we will look at a stress management program called Relaxation Technique. This technique can help calm nerves, reduce muscle tension and help boost your health.

Relaxation techniques include a number of practices such as *progressive relaxation, guided imagery, biofeedback, self-hypnosis, and deep breathing exercises*. The goal is similar in all: to produce the body's natural relaxation response characterized by slower breathing, lower blood pressure, and a feeling of increased well-being.

Meditation and practices that include *meditation* with movements, such as yoga and tai chi can also promote relaxation. You can find information about these practices elsewhere on the NCCIH Website.

Stress management programs commonly include relaxation techniques. Relaxation techniques have also been studied to see whether they might be of value in managing various health problems.

"Always give yourself time to relax; even 15 minutes of alone time can do wonders. Never neglect your needs, remember you are as important as the people you love." - Rubyanne

The best kind of pampering is when you pamper yourself.

Health benefits of relaxation

They say a dose of everything is good but too much of it is bad, and the same goes for stress. When you are stressed, it can result in health issues like dementia or high blood pressure if not controlled.

CBS reported on a small study that examined the role of stress in seizures and found that people are often misdiagnosed with epilepsy while learning helpful relaxation and coping techniques may be a better solution.

There are various health benefits of relaxation and they include:

- Prevents health issues

Issues such as Dementia, High Blood Pressure, and Headache can easily be prevented if we don't stress ourselves and these issues cause financial crisis because they drain your account. Living a stress-free life can then be inferred to be economical and make you live longer.

- Keeps you from isolation

When a person thinks too much, he/she tends to forget where they are thereby isolating themselves from other people and as this continues, you will see yourself gradually letting go of people and things that matter to you.

According to researcher John Cacioppo at the University of Chicago, 20 percent of all people are unhappy because of social isolation at any given moment. For decades now, researchers have tracked the effects of loneliness and isolation on our physical health.

Another study found that isolation is a risk factor for disease on par with smoking and obesity. Loneliness often leads to stress, which is a risk factor for many conditions in its own right.

- Helps us think clearer

According to a 2012 study, it was found out that stress seems to actually change how we weigh risks and rewards and can cloud our judgment when we are faced with important decisions.

Relaxation is better for our health and because it calms our nerves and mind, it makes us point out our problems and proffer solutions with a clearer mind which causes us to make good decisions.

- Fertility

<u>Research</u> suggests women are more likely to conceive when they're relaxed as opposed to when they're stressed.

- Healthy body

There are various relaxation exercises that you can do to calm your nerves such as yoga, stretches and breathing control. These exercises restore energy and encourage positivity.

Chapter 5: Staying Energized At Work And Your Life

"Energy is the ability to shape the world"—Anonymous

Aside from the main point which is it yields productivity when you are energized, you are active and ready to take over the world, and this is why they say it is better to start a project when we are at our energy peak. It is amazing how much we are ready to tackle when our blood is pumping so much to spill information on something we want to do. However, we cannot always have the zeal to be so happy and ready to conquer situations and that is why I will be pointing out 5 ways to stay energized. There are, of course, other ways to stay energized and they are equally important.

Ways to Stay Energized

- Eat and drink sugar

The fact that doing things are okay but when you do them too much is when it becomes uncomfortable and a health issue if not controlled. This cannot be overemphasized and it also applies to sugar which is very important and provides energy to the body.

- Take a cold shower

A cold shower calms your nerves and helps you to think, so make it a way to relax and become energized. After a stressful activity, we are always advised to take a cold shower because we become refreshed afterward and think clearer.

- Eat vitamins

This is one of the nutrients contained to make a balanced diet because it is essential in ensuring our health is not at stake. There are supplements that contain these nutrients so that it will not be avoided. Some of these vitamin nutrients are:

1. Omega 3 which is an essential fatty acid and important for brain health. Lack of Omega 3 can result in fatigue or depression.
2. Vitamin B is essential for the formation of the red blood cells and can be found in a lot of energy drinks.

3. Vitamin C can help protect the body from immune deficiencies, other health issues and increase our energy level. This is why doctors always prescribe Vitamin C to patients at almost every doctor's appointment.

- Reduce your caffeine intake

The US Food and Drug Administration (FDA) states that the average amount of caffeine consumed in the US is approximately 300 mg per person per day, equivalent to between two and four cups of coffee. This is considered to be a moderate caffeine intake, which according to many studies can promote a variety of health benefits.

However, <u>The Mayo Clinic states that</u> consuming more than 500-600 mg of caffeine a day may lead to insomnia, nervousness, restlessness, irritability, an upset stomach, a fast heartbeat and even muscle tremors.

Caffeine is a central nervous system stimulant that causes alertness when it reaches the brain and the stimulant can be found in coffee or energy drink. It is advisable, to be cautious by substituting with cold drinks.

- Flexibility

Whatever you do, move! Flexibility gets blood and oxygen flowing in your muscle and stretching the body can help release tension and aid energy.

A landmark study published in Journal of Personality and Social Psychology revealed that a brisk 10-minute walk can have a revitalizing effect, enhancing energy for at least two hours.

Importance of Staying Energized

Energy is important to humans and plants because it helps sustain life and it helps the cells as they cannot perform on their own. Energy is power and we need it to grow, to function properly and maintain balance.

It is important you stay energized as it helps you to refocus and achieve your target aim for the day.

It is also important to chew a stick of gum, as a 2015 U.K. study found that this trick raised alertness and improved concentration, possibly because chewing increases blood flow.

Ways to Stay Energized at Work

We wake up fresh in the morning and get drained towards the afternoon which is normal as the body and brain gets tired. We get tired but there are various ways we can refresh ourselves to remain active and alert all through the day and they include:

- Take activity break

You should know your energy peak and when it falters. This will enable you to know when you should be a critical thinker and when you should just relax. However, you should always take an activity break because the mind wanders when you are focused on something for too long. Go over to your colleague's desk and talk a little or stretch a little; this will help the mind refocus and ready to think well again.

- Keep snacks handy

It is important to have healthy snacks at hand; it will not only help you with hunger but will also keep you energized and productive.

Green tea, dark chocolate, vegetable e salad, almonds, and chickpeas are some of the snacks one can eat to quiet those inner monsters and remain healthy.

Balancing out your lunch/snacks, instead of just eating leftover pasta can have a big impact on your day, according to the Harvard School of Public Health Nutrition Source.

- Stay hydrated

Water makes up 72% of the body and is a source of lubricant the body needs to maintain body temperature, joint tissues, and waste product.

Drink a lot of water to keep your body active and hydrated as pure water is the World's first and foremost medicine. - **Slovakian Proverb**

In case you don't like the taste of pure water, there are other fluids to drink like milk, hot or cold tea or juice, but they have to be moderate because of the additional ingredients in them and for health purposes.

- Get enough sleep

When you stay rested, you wake up better and full of energy making you go a long way to increase productivity at work. Sleep is very important for health and prevents sickness like heart disease, depression, headache, stroke and many more. Try to take a minimum of 5 hours sleep as an adult for your mental health and for repair of body tissues.

- Stare Off into Space

Staring at a computer screen for hours on end really strains the eyes and worsens exhaustion. Keep the 20-20-20 rule in mind when you are feeling a bit lackluster by looking at a point that is 20 feet away, for 20 seconds, every 20 minutes to break the continuous computer screen fixation.

How to Stay Energized at Home

It's one thing to be energized at work to be productive in what you do; it's another to be energetic at home. In order not to be bored at home, you need to go out and remain active in what you do. There are ways to remain energized at home and they include:

- Go out for some fresh air

Sometimes, a cool fresh air is all you need to remain calm and be active. Air is important in breathing that reproduces energy for the body.

- Give yourself something to look forward to

When you give yourself something to look forward to, it motivates you to have an inspiration in the project or activity ahead of you and it energizes you, knowing you have ideas you want to lay down and conquer.

- Socialize

Go out, make new friends and most importantly, enjoy yourself. This helps to calm your nerves and makes you freer. Socialization is very important in life as it makes you get to know people and have ideas of other people's perspective. It is interesting how you learn a lot when you are with people and most importantly, being with people can energize you.

You can't stay in your corner of the forest waiting for others to meet you. You have to go to them sometimes.

- Exercise

It can't be overly emphasized that exercise is a good stress reliever; it is not only a stress reliever but good for the health. There are various exercises for the mind to help improve memory and thinking skills that will help to calm the nerves.

In <u>a study done at the University of British Columbia</u>, researchers found that regular aerobic exercise, the kind that gets your heart and your sweat glands pumping, appears to boost the size of the hippocampus, the brain area involved in verbal memory and learning.

- Read

Reading sharpens the mind and helps you process information. Read books to engage and energize your mind and mental being. It is therapeutic, good for analytical thinking, expands your vocabulary and helps to appreciate others.

A recent study found that people who read are two and a half times less likely to be diagnosed with Alzheimer's Syndrome later on in life. Although this does not mean that reading will prevent the disease, it proves a slight relationship between reading and prevention.

<u>According to</u> Cristel Russell, a behavioral researcher, reading can help with any stress or turmoil occurring in your life. If you're going through a break-up, or simply just need to relax, try a new book.

Chapter 6: Stress And Success

***"Success is not measured in the achievement of goals, but in the stress and strain of meeting those goals".—* Spencer W. Kimball**

Pioneering research using brain scanners has located the worry center of the brain and suggests for the first time that it is an area involved in survival and the assessment of threats and risks.

The hippocampus plays a role in the fight-or-flight response by triggering physiological changes including a tensing of muscles ready for action and a faster heartbeat to get more blood flowing to the brain and muscles.

Stress is the body's way of reacting to threat or situations around you that are not clear. Anxiety is an absolutely necessary emotion and it is important to control and channel it to the right direction so that we can grow.

Stress isn't always bad, in small doses, it can help you perform under pressure and motivate you to do your best but when it goes overboard it causes health issues and some symptoms that lead to stress include headache, low energy, body pain or even insomnia.

However, what is stressful to you might not be stressful to the next person so it is important to know your stress tolerance level and how to control it and most importantly, relax.

What makes us stressed?

- The picture of wanting to be perfect

The World has a specific definition of perfect and that is what causes peer pressure and stress in youths, generally because they are influenced or want to be this "PERFECT" people talk about and this causes stress.

- Life worries

Moving elsewhere is one of the most stressful events you will experience in your life. More generally, any situation which requires change, positive or negative, requires us to adapt to new circumstances and can be a source of stress.

Thomas Holmes and Richard Rahe produced an inventory of life-changing events known as the Social Readjustment Rating Scale (SRRS) which, surprisingly, ranks the act of moving home as the 28th most stressful life change. Far more severe are changes in relationships, such as a partner's death or separation (Holmes and Rahe, 1967).

- Financial obligations

Financial issues are another way a person can worry because it can lead to unnecessary stress which can be a burden to yourself and those close to you. We will always need money for something, e.g. bills, house rent, food, outing, petrol etc. even if we save enough, emergencies will always come around and we will see our self-taking loans.

Kanner's Hassles Scale found that a feeling of not being able to pay bills and live comfortably, as well as the burden of supporting others financially to be a key strain in our everyday lives (Kanner et al, 1981).

- Health issues

Fears over one's health or the wellbeing of a relative or friend are a common cause of stress. The experience of an illness, and the loss of control over events can lead to persistent worry about both the current and possible future situations.

- Past events

Past events can be a key source of stress because the trauma of the past can continue to affect people many years after. The U.S. Department of Veteran Affairs estimates that around 50% of women experience a traumatic event at least once in their life, and are more prone to becoming victims of sexual violence than men. However, 60% of men also experience trauma, a difference which it attributes to males being more likely to be involved in accidents.

We become stressed because of the situations around us, the overwhelming need to achieve a measurable height for our self which brings about success.

<u>According to a University of Florida psychologist,</u> Tim Judge and his colleagues have shown overwhelmingly that people who feel that they control the events in their lives (more than the events control them) and are confident in their abilities end up doing better on nearly every important measure of work performance.

Successful people are goal-oriented, they know what they want and they go for it. They are risk-takers, patient and focused, you also have to be determined to work harder than before and more than your peers to achieve your target. Success takes hard- work, self-motivation and learning more to be willing to sacrifice.

When you achieve your desired goal and the impact is measurable, it is said you are a success. It is not by having a plan but identifying it and knowing the steps to take to make it implementable and reaching the result. If you are not focused on a positive mindset, you might not achieve the goal set by you or for you.

It is important to be successful in life because it gives you a level of confidence, security, and a sense of well-being, the ability to contribute at a greater level, hope and leadership. Without it, your goals and dreams are just abstract.

To be successful, you need to have various traits and attributes to build that confidence and target you will need to achieve those goals. There are various ways you can arrive at your final destination but it is not all rosy and you need commitment and drive to get there.

There are various ways to go to be successful and some of them are:

- Having a personal goal and aiming to achieve them

When you achieve just one important goal in life, your subconscious mind will always look in that direction creating a pattern for you to continue in that direction and it helps build your confidence and belief that you will be successful in what you set out to achieve.

In other words, you learn to succeed by succeeding and the more you achieve, the more you can achieve.

- Unlimited potential

Doing the best at this moment puts you in the best place for the next moment. **Oprah Winfrey**

The only real limits on what you can do, have or be, are self-imposed, once you know what you want, you can achieve it with hard work and determination as long as you do not stop.

- Focus on the journey, not the destination

Focus on the little things that make the big picture, if you continually look at the goal and not what will make the goal be accomplished, it will remain abstract. Also, fuel your mind with knowledge so you can understand how to get to your destination. Keep thinking about what you are learning and see what you can improve.

- Get rid of stagnating thoughts.

Thoughts influence feelings and feelings determine how you view your work. When you have a lot in your head, it is difficult to pick the positive thoughts to manifest in, thereby making you lose focus and in doubt.

- Plan

It is important to have a plan for the activities you want to render for the goal you want to achieve. It is less stressful and very organized when you have a detailed idea of how you want to execute your task, giving you room to think of other ideas to add to execute your project remarkably. Planning is time-conscious and saves decision-making muscles for more important activities.

Is stress useful for Success?

A survey by TalentSmart showed that 90 percent of top performers know how to manage their emotions in times of stress so that they remain cool, calm, and able to do what needs to be done.

Worrying too much leads to depression or memory loss but an adequate amount of it leads to you trying to make things work and this leads to success or progress at it may be.

Finally, without stress or worry or anxiety, we would not make an extra mile move to do more. Stress helps us make actions we will not necessarily take cognizance of; it is also used to prompt a specific action, to a specific threat, or to promote alertness during a brief period of danger.

A line between stress and success

If you can't handle stress, then you can't handle success. – The Millionaire's Club

There is a thin line between getting anxious, then worried, and being successful. This is because stress is a feeling in your head that causes tension when being pressured into doing or accomplishing something. On the other hand, success is that fulfilling attainment of accomplishing a said target.

It is human to always want more from life; we are not satisfied with what we have, so we think of ways to achieve other things and also as humans, our stress processor ticks in when the fear of the unknown is brought about until they are resolved. Research has shown that some stress is good for us, it helps us perform at optimal levels but too much stress can have serious psychological and physiological effects on the body and mind.

According to a study: Employees at a financial institution were asked to take a test on their stress mindset before and after watching three videos over the course of a week that either presented stress as enhancing or harmful. In a second study, students who had previously taken a survey on their stress mindset were told in class that five of them would be randomly selected to give a speech that would also be videotaped. For each student, mouth swabs were taken to measure cortisol levels. Each was also asked to decide if chosen to speak, whether or not they would receive feedback from their peers and business school experts who watched the footage.

The findings: In the first study, not only were many people influenced by the message of the videos, those who viewed the video and approached stress as enhancing, reported better work performance, as well as less psychological complications. As for the students, those who naturally saw stress as helpful had a more moderate cortisol response upon hearing about the speech possibility and they were more likely to request feedback.

In conclusion, stress is an outburst that leads to success although it has to be controlled so that we may not have so many thoughts that can deprive us of our goal. If we don't stress, we will not be able to strive so hard to accomplish our set goal and that is where the line comes in. Stress can be a positive factor in success and can also be a negative factor.

Facts about Stress

- According to a survey conducted by the American Psychological Association in 2010, these five factors

are the reasons for stress in America: money, work, relationships, family and economic.
- While it is a myth that stress can turn hair grey, it can cause hair loss. In fact, hair loss can begin up to three months after a stressful event.
- Bullying, child abuse, and stress cause children to age faster at a cellular level and leads to physical and mental health problems even decades later, including an earlier death.
- Acne breakouts can occur in some people, while others might have itchy rashes. Both symptoms are related to an inflammatory response from stress.
- You are who you hang out with. Give up on toxic people and surround yourself with a positive, diverse and open-minded crowd. You will most likely also adopt a positive outlook on life.
- Stress and lack of sleep are the biggest enemies of a healthy, happy person. Don't work towards success at the price of your health, you'll regret it.
- Success is relative. Your benchmark for success is different from someone else's and will probably change quite a few

times. Try to make a note of what your benchmark is (write it down if you must) so you can give yourself the kudos you deserve when you achieve it.

Chapter 7: Leveraging Stress For A Happier Life

"The greatest weapon against stress is our ability to choose one thought over another"—William James

In 2012, Harvard School of Public Health conducted an analysis that indicated that there is a connection between our mood and our state of health. Experts have been warning the public for so many years now about the hazards associated with stress. They have found out that there is a relationship between stress and health issues like heart disease, headaches, depression, and diabetes. The warnings have, however, not done much to suppress the incidence of stress. In America for instance, there has been a surge in the incidence of stress in recent years.

Individuals studying this have postulated that the increase in stress could be a result of several factors such as money, work, relationships, and the general air of politics that permeates many societies. The 2015 Healthline survey indicates that these factors cause at least 60% of stress in the US. Fair enough.

They say if you cannot beat them, join them. Researchers have now decided to turn their focus to something strange and even more interesting a line of study—the beauty of stress. Could stress actually offer anything good? They have found something shocking—stress actually has its own set of benefits—it enhances your body systems to work stronger, faster, and with more energy.

It is not strange to hear that people love success, and some, as much as they love happiness. To some, happiness is a life free of stress, fears, and worries. Well, we shall soon find out what real happiness is about.

The Meaning of Happiness and Success

It is not easy to give a specific definition to these notions; in fact, they are subjective to some extent. You personally have to ask yourself what success and happiness means to you. Some people might say its academic accomplishment, to some it is money, and to some others, it is something different. But there is not one generally acceptable standard of success.

And as for happiness, it would be too narrow as well to ascribe money or material possessions as the source of happiness. The thing about happiness is that no one has a monopoly on it; you can experience it if you let yourself. You have the autonomic right to decide if stress should deprive you of happiness or if it should engineer it. Before we discuss that, we quickly look at the key factors that fundamentally propel happiness.

- Gratitude

We must be appreciative of what we already have for us to enjoy success and happiness. It is important to know that happiness is principal and success, in fact, hangs upon it. What are our biggest desires and dreams? Are we accomplishing them? If your answer to the last question is in the affirmative, then chances are that you are living a happy life, and chances are even more that you are living a life of success.

Take out some time to write down everything you have accomplished, all the things you are grateful for, even the air you still have flowing through your nostrils. Express some gratitude, think of the many worse situations you could have been in, and prove to yourself that many people would pay to be in your royal shoes. There has been something you are grateful for, at least that you can read this book is a gift you might not realize the worth of at this time. Appreciate the miracles of the universe and the gigantic design that went into your biological formation.

- Live Today

You have lived yesterday and you are yet to live tomorrow, do not be distracted from living today. The German physicist Albert Einstein once said, "I don't worry much about the future, for it comes soon enough." We are often trapped in our worries about the past and future that we forget to do the things we ought to do in the present.

Yes, there may be problems that cause us to stray us away from living each moment to the fullest, but those problems make life. They are characteristic of our reality and no one can promise their absence. However, we must know that we are bigger than our problems and they should not weigh us down. Problems shape us, yes, they can cause agony and pains, and they teach us wisdom although they can cause us daunting times — they have their good sides as well, just like stress. Know this and let it guide you through the paths that that would take you to the doors of triumph.

- Good Time Management

There are great chances that your success and happiness are linked to how well you manage time. As a time manager, you set your priorities right, you know what you should do every moment and what you should forgo for what. You should keep the things that have an overall positive impact on your goals at the top of your schedule. Look carefully and monitor your long-term goals and take those activities that would enhance their accomplishment.

The consequence of not managing your time well is that you fall prey to the harassment of stressors and other agents of anxiety. We mix up some activities as a result of the haphazard organization of our schedule in our minds. Eventually, you get the feeling that you have not accomplished all that you ought to; by accumulating this feeling over time, you feel stressed and unhappy.

We all have the same amount of time in a day—its 24 hours—what differentiates us is how we use our time. Do we play golf when we have a board meeting to attend?

- Pursue the right goals

Often, what holds us back from achieving success in life, whatever we might define that as, is our inability to set goals the right way. In a recent study, it was determined that only 8% of people who set goals on New Year's Eve actually achieve them. But beyond just those New Year's goals, we all know that many people often set goals but don't achieve them.

Surely, you've set a goal in the past and you gave up on it. All of us have. But, it's the goal-setting process that got in the way. When we set passive goals, in that we don't actually set the goals on paper and don't define them out in detail, nor create a plan for their attainment, we tend to either fail or give up on it. But for people who set goals the right way, success is far more attainable.

When you set SMARTER goals, you're setting Specific (S), Meaningful (M), Achievable (A), Relevant (R), and Time-Based (T) goals that are Evaluated (E), and the approach is Re-Adjusted (R) until you succeed. This is an important process in the success recipe and people who don't follow along find goal achievement far more difficult.

If you want to set SMARTER goals, grab a sheet of paper and start writing. It won't work without writing it out. What do you want? Specifically, what do you want? Describe it in great detail. Don't leave any stone unturned. Don't just say you want millions of dollars or to be skinny. Say an exact number of dollars and an exact number of pounds or kilos that you want to lose, with a specific date for its achievement.

As long as these goals are meaningful, in that they aren't just superficial goals, and you have some driving force behind them that's bigger than you, then you're part of the way there. And, by achievable, we're not trying to discourage lofty goals. But you also don't want to set yourself up for disappointment by saying you want to make a billion dollars in 12 months, especially if you're currently heavily in debt, for example.

- **Start your day on the right foot**

As the sunrise in the east, let your dawn set in with a spark of light. The things you do in the morning set the pace for the rest of the day. In turn, it dictates the outcome of your life. If you want to be happy and successful, create a set of habits in the morning to help foster that in your life. The right combination of habits executed day-in and day-out can make all the difference.

We're such creatures of habit that we forget to do the things that will benefit our lives because we get caught up doing the things that we're so used to. We're steeped in habit and routine, and not necessarily ones that serve us. Usually, we're too busy responding to life and its overwhelming demands on us, in order to take the bulls by the horn, so to speak.

But if we want to get ahead, succeed, and feel mentally at peace with ourselves, we need an empowering morning routine. These good morning habits need to be front-loaded at the start of the day because that's when our minds are so fresh and we have so much clarity. And, by waking up early enough to tackle a list of good habits, we're setting ourselves up for success and happiness.

Create a routine that will help empower your life rather than hinder it. Wake up early, eat a good breakfast, work out for 20 minutes, do yoga or meditate, write out a set of daily goals, and so on. Don't live life in neutral. Take control, grab the reins, and be inspired and motivated to do and achieve something while helping others and yourself in the process.

- **Never Joke about your important daily activities**

MIT is an acronym for *most important tasks*, and they form an integral part of success. They offer one of the most crucial keys to achieving our goals in life over the long term. It's not always easy to go after the MITs, especially when we feel so stressed out or overwhelmed by life. But it's a necessary act if we're going to get where we need to go.

Going about identifying your MITs is a crucial part of this process. In time management, we call these quadrant-two activities — the important but not urgent things necessary to achieve your long-term goals. Once you've identified your MITs, chase after them first thing in the morning. Once your empowering morning routine is completed, get to these first.

Every single day, there's some action, big or small, that we can take to help advance us towards our goals. As long as you can identify those, and you can implement those actions day after day, you can succeed in time. The biggest problem? It won't happen overnight. And that's where most people get frustrated with things.

Make a list the night before of your MITs that you want to tackle the next day. Then, when you wake up the following day, ensure that you get after that list. Keep the list handy with you throughout your morning routine and focus on the MITs once it's complete. Don't start your "busy work" that day until you get the MITs out of the way.

- **Don't compromise on Health**

Health and wellbeing are an important part of the happiness-and-success formula, and one of the biggest keys to achieving them both. When we do things to harm ourselves by overeating, over-drinking alcohol, taking recreational drugs, and the like, not only does it have an adverse effect on our bodies, but also on our minds.

The chemical makeup and neurochemistry of the brain, which will excrete stress hormones when we tax the body with substance abuse or don't take care of the way we look by indulging in a variety of hedonistic pleasures, can alter our motivation and desire to improve our lives. While it's okay to indulge every now and then in certain pleasures, for the most part, people have difficulty quitting while they're ahead.

The overall focus has to be on health. The day needs to start and end healthy. It doesn't mean that life has to be boring. But if you want to get ahead, be happy and successful, you need to ensure that you're putting the right things into your body. Clean body, clean mind. That's how it goes. From lean proteins to reduced caloric intakes, non-alcoholic and non-carbonated drinks, and less-fatty foods, we need to focus on what goes in, whether it's solid or liquid.

We also need to get grounded mentally. We need to do things like meditate and relax the mind. Take up a yoga class or institute an exercise regimen so that you have something that starts incorporating healthy habits into your life. It isn't easy. But it does get easier over time as long you continue to repeat the right behaviors.

Leveraging on Stress to improve productivity

So, having known that stress can help you, noting the distinction between "stress" and "overstress", the next natural thing is how stress can help you accomplish happiness. We consider some ways by which you can gain from your stress, so that when you feel stressed out next time; you would see the opportunities in it before you fall prey to anxiety.

More precisely, there is *Eustress* and *Distress,* and it is distress which wears you down and causes the heart attacks and weight gains. The former is, however, a positive sort of stress that gives you energy and enhances your productivity. But to a large extent, it depends on you what kind of stress a stress would be—whether positive or negative. Some people love challenges and look to tackling time-bound tasking exercises, while others dread such situations; it's a relative kind of phenomenon.

You must learn first to own your stress and manage it accordingly, that is the first step to attaining a comfortable life despite the spites of stress. Yes, butterflies in your stomach and other nervous activities might not land you in the hospital bed, but they can do so over a long time span. Now, it becomes more dangerous when you try to help yourself out with drugs and alcohol. Below we consider five strategies for making a positive life out of a stress-filled life.

➢ Raise your Guts over your Fears

Life throws a lot of challenges our way, but how should we respond? You must not give in—you never back down. The more you realize that you are in control, the less the effects of stress become pronounced. Yes, your palms may be drooling a bucket of sweats, and your heart racing so significantly to beat a drum on your chest, relax and be in charge—the motto is *guts over fears*. Your system even gets better when you let the adrenaline flow through. The idea is not to act afraid.

➢ Be Optimistic

Expect the best from life and keep your thinking positive. However, it is important that you prepare well enough to grab any opportunity that comes your way. No matter the task and the deadlines you need to meet, just do your homework and never forget your onions, and you are good. In as much as you are prepared, you should keep your expectations positive, and the best is sure to smile your way. That is just the principle; work hard and retain a good hope. Note that you must do your part, it does not happen from anything.

➢ Have a Conversation with yourself

Do this often, especially in your downtimes. Make yourself see the magic in you. Tell yourself words of encouragement, things like "I can make it", "I can in fact do this!", and "I've worked on more demanding challenges, so this one is child's play." By so doing, you reassure yourself of the potentials you carry and it elevates you to launch into the successful spot you seek.

> ➢ Know that nobody is perfect and failure is another chance to succeed

This is where you should demonstrate some critical understanding. Millennials are sometimes convinced that they can easily attain perfection. Perfection is not the target; the best is ok. You must not accept that you failed; you simply missed your shot and will re-fire. You must not give up on yourself for any reason.

> ➢ Enjoy your breathing rhythm

This method has proven very instrumental in calming wandering minds effectively. Relax and count your breaths one after one, and don't lose focus.

Conclusion

Stress is the way your body responds to any form of threat and this is because as humans, we have a defense mechanism that allows us to fight battles of the past, present or future. There are various situations that lead to stress such as work, traffic, financial obligations, health issues, family and friends and a host of other things. These situations stress us and make us ill, leading to emotional problems such as anger, depression or even low self-esteem.

Stress and anxiety go hand in hand and the reaction from anxiety is what brings about stress. Stress is a silent killer and can lead to various health problems such as high blood pressure, chest pain or irregular heartbeat amongst others. Stress can come in various forms, both mentally or physically.

Some facts about stress include:

- A CNN poll reveals that the number one reason for stress in most countries is money. The countries most stressed about money are Malaysia, China,

Singapore, and the United States. The countries least stressed about money are Russia, France, and Italy.
- Pupils dilate (mydriasis) during stress much the same way they dilate in response to attraction: to gather more visual information about a situation.
- Research has shown that dark chocolate reduces stress hormones such as cortisol and other fight-flight hormones. Additionally, cocoa is rich in antioxidants called flavonoids.
- Stress can alter blood sugar levels, which can cause mood swings, fatigue, hyperglycemia, and metabolic syndrome, a major risk factor for heart attack and diabetes.
- <u>Stress increases the risk of pre-term labor</u> and intrauterine infection. Additionally, chronic levels of stress place a fetus at greater risk for developing stress-related disorders and affect the fetus's temperament and neurobehavioral development.

You can reduce stress by exercising, relaxing, eating healthy, being creative and meditating. These ways help calm the mind and energize the body making you happy and at peace.

These ways also help to task the mind and increase productivity, however, if you do pay so much attention to stress, you will end up isolating yourself or having health issues. Some of the symptoms of stress include depression, heart disease, headache, and body pain amongst others. To avoid this in the workplace and in your life, it is important to stay hydrated, move around, socialize and read. Once you have successfully done all these, you are sure of having a success-filled life.

Copyright © 2018 by Pollux Andrews
All rights reserved. No part of this book may be reproduced in any form without permission in writing from the author.

No part of this publication may be reproduced or transmitted in any form or by any means, mechanical or electronic, including photocopying or recording, or by any information storage and retrieval system, or transmitted by email or by any other means whatsoever without permission in writing from the author.

DISCLAIMER

While all attempts have been made to verify the information provided in this publication, the author does not assume any responsibility for errors, omissions, or contrary interpretations of the subject matter herein.

The views expressed are those of the author alone and should not be taken as expert instruction or commands. The reader is responsible for his or her own actions.

The author makes no representations or warranties with respect to the accuracy or completeness of the contents of this work and specifically disclaims all warranties, including without limitation warranties of fitness for a particular purpose. No warranty may be created or extended by sales or promotional materials. The advice and recipes contained herein may not be suitable for everyone. This work is sold with the understanding that the author is not engaged in rendering medical, legal or other professional advice or services. If professional assistance is required, the services of a competent professional person should be sought. The author shall not be liable for damages arising here from. The fact that an individual, organization of website is referred to in this work as a citation and/or potential source of further information does not mean that the author endorses the information the individual, organization to website may provide or recommendations they/it may make. Further, readers should be aware that Internet websites listed in this work might have changed or disappeared between when this work was written and when it is read.

Adherence to all applicable laws and regulations, including international, federal, state, and local governing professional licensing, business practices, advertising, and all other aspects of doing business in any jurisdiction in the world is the sole responsibility of the purchaser or reader.

www.ingramcontent.com/pod-product-compliance
Lightning Source LLC
Chambersburg PA
CBHW031925240526
45464CB00022B/897